Saigon Street Colloquial Vietnamese Slang Swearing

by Elly Thuy Nguyen

Copyright 2015 by Elly Thuy Nguyen

Volume 4 of the My Saigon series written by Elly Thuy Nguyen, all available on Amazon.com

Saigon Street Talk

Introduction..3
Safety warning..6
Building blocks of Vietnamese context: terms of address............7
9x youth slang..9
Swearing: the bad stuff..16
Types of people...20
Business..24
Love, sex, relationships...26
High school...29

Introduction

I love the Vietnamese language. And while I've studied and learned formal and literary Vietnamese, what most excites me is street Vietnamese, the language you hear on the streets of Saigon. It's colorful and fun, and I don't know of any reference for it, not even in Vietnamese language. You just have to know it if you know it, or collect it from overheard conversations in person or online. I wrote this book to collect and present to you colloquial slang Vietnamese, as spoken in Saigon in 2015.

Whether you are a traveler to Vietnam, a scholar or student of Vietnamese, a Vietkieu (ethnically Vietnamese person living outside Vietnam), or even a native speaker of Vietnamese, this book will give you deep knowledge of contemporary Vietnamese slang. Most Vietnamese native speakers don't know *all* the slang in this guide, and my friends and I have had fun learning and using some of the expressions in this guide that are novel to us. They are amazingly colorful and evocative, and often tell stories in themselves. Vietnamese culture has a natural love of wordplay, and touchy subjects are often discussed in creatively metaphorical ways.

Slang is cutting-edge and open-source, created on the street, and always reflecting the *zeitgeist*. That's not so easy in a country like Vietnam, where the social and political culture both don't prize complete openness about feelings, and some popular feelings are popularly left mostly unsaid. A lot of those unsaid feelings are put out in slang, even youth slang. Consider this guide not just a list of words, but a list of Vietnamese people's thoughts, feelings, hopes, and fears, in 2015.

But be careful. using slang can be a touchy matter. Even if the expression is not in itself offensive, in Vietnamese culture, as you might already know, using an informal expression in a formal setting can cause offense. This is true in any culture, but most likely much more true in Vietnamese culture than in Western cultures. I know that in the US you don't say "what's up man" to a court judge sitting in front of you, but doing so would not be completely unheard of, nor bring the likely grave consequences it would bring in Vietnam. So the point here is be careful when you use any terms you're not careful about, and ask your Vietnamese friends for additional context-specific guidance to supplement what I've provided in this book.

This book assumes that you can pronounce Vietnamese words without my assistance. If you can't, there are plentiful online (or human) resources to teach you how to do that. I don't want to bog this book down (hey, there's some American slang!) with basic Vietnamese phonography. Similarly, this book assumes that you have some source to go to for standard office or school Vietnamese. Please don't let this book be your only source of the Vietnamese language, because you'll end up sounding like a parrot who hung out on the wrong side of the tracks!

About tones: most Vietnamese language courses emphasize that you learn the tones first. That is absolutely correct if your goal is fluency or proficiency. Without tones, you'll be speaking broken, pidgin-ish Vietnamese. But the key thing those other courses forget to tell you is: people will still almost always understand you. In most contexts, it's clear which tone you mean, even if you said the wrong one. Tone-learning advocates point out that the word "pho," with a tone that does not correspond to the expected meaning of "soup," can carry the literal meaning of, for example, "town." Fine. But how likely is it that a restaurant waiter will be perplexed about why you just ordered a bowl of town, and stand staring at you in incomprehension? Similarly, a Vietnamese person who goes to the United States may go to a McDonalds and order a "chi bu ga," and the McDonalds employee will not stand there wondering what in the world a "chi bu ga" is, because this person's pronunciation wasn't exactly perfect! So if you don't mind sounding like Ms. "chi bu ga" in Vietnam -- say if you are only a short-term visitor -- then I'm going to tell you what almost no other Vietnamese language guide will tell you, and I will advise you not to worry about the tones, at least not for now. They require too much effort to master, and can be a turn-off for someone new to the language.

Additionally to this, street Vietnamese, like colloquial street language in any country, is often slurred, misspoken, mispronounced, ungrammatical, and given and received over the din of clinking coffee glasses and starting motorcycles. It's meant to be understood perfectly well even without correct pronunciation. To go back to our imaginary Vietnamese tourist in the United States, if this Vietnamese tourist is angry at you for overcharging her for a chi bu ga, and with her imperfect English yells that you are a "fokker," (which is in fact how Vietnamese people tend to say that word) would you stand there wondering "Why does she think I am a Dutch aerospace firm?" or would you know exactly what she meant?

So there. Tones are important for achieving proficient Vietnamese pronunciation, but if you're just a beginner or just a visitor, it's better to be having fun with the language rather than worrying about tones -- and as you become more familiar with your first attempts at the language, the tones will likely come to you naturally as part of the pronunciation.

While I don't suggest you fret about tones, I do suggest you get some idea of how to pronounce Vietnamese consonants. It's not identical to Roman-alphabet pronunciation, and that might throw you off. For example, there are two types of letter D, one pronounced like y as in yankee, and the other pronounced like you expect D to be pronounced. Wikipedia and many other sources can give you tables of how to pronounce Vietnamese letters; the information is not difficult to find online. Make sure you're using Saigon pronouncation. If there are z sounds (if you ever see the pronunciation directive "as in *zebra*"), you've got Hanoi pronunciation, which is not how this Saigon slang was intended to be pronounced.

Pronunciation guides are easy, but there's no other compendium of Vietnamese slang out there, especially not in English. I've worked hard putting it together for you, and I learned a lot about my native language in the process. I hope you enjoy this very special book.

-Elly

Safety warning

I've alluded to this already, and I'm going to put it very plainly right here:

BE CAREFUL when using any of the terms in this book with people who aren't trusted friends of yours.

I've intentionally separated the really bad profanity into its own chapter, but still, be careful using anything from this book when you're not certain of the situation.

Street language can often have wildly different meanings and contexts, and saying something with the wrong look, even if it's normally only a "mild" profanity, might lead to very bad consequences. That's true in Vietnam only as much as it's true anywhere else in the world. But I'm pointing this out to you because this is really a no-holds-barred book of Vietnamese slang. My friends advised me to leave out the really rude stuff, because it might get my foreign readers into trouble, but I want to bring you all the Vietnamese that's out there -- even if I really don't advise you to try using it with random strangers until you're very familiar with it.

Vietnamese and American children are both taught this as a Chinese proverb, but I like to think that it's a Vietnamese insight: *when the word is in your mouth, it is your slave, but once it is out of your mouth, you are its slave.*

Be careful.

Building blocks of Vietnamese context: terms of address

You may already know that regular Vietnamese, of the kind you might use in an office or school, doesn't really use a first-person or second-person. In normal speech, we use third-person terms, based on familial relationships, where other languages use the first-person or second-person. So for example instead of saying "I like you," you would say something in Vietnamese that parsed by word-for-word translation would come out to (for example) "Younger sibling likes older brother" (if you're speaking to a man about your age or slightly older). And so on with all pronouns. They are replaced by generally rather polite terms corresponding to family relationships. The most frequently used are "anh," "chị," and "em" -- for, respectively, older brother, older sister, and younger sibling. There is a vast trove of other terms of address, including some used only in literary or ancient (royal) contexts, and what is important for you to know is that these terms of address are the most important signifiers of tone, attitude, and respect in Vietnamese language.

While office and school Vietnamese uses a set of respectful familial kinship-related pronouns, street Vietnamese doesn't always do so. Yes, even in the roughest street situations, you *can* use the regular, "office Vietnamese" terms. But you don't have to. The street equivalents are a lot more direct. They closely correspond to the idea of first-person, second-person, and generic third-person in other languages, because they don't differentiate by status and age. But in Vietnamese, ignoring status and age is in itself already either rude or very familiar. In general, using these terms, rather than the textbook kinship terms, is seen as aggressive and arrogant. The closest equivalent I can think of in English is pointing your finger at someone and saying "hey you!" These words are the most surefire way to be rude in Vietnamese, and you can make a polite statement rude by switching from anh/chị/em to these terms. On the other hand, like many "rude" terms, they can be used by close friends, either as joking insults (the same way you might call your friend the worst English profanities), or just as a show of informality.

First person (I): **tao**

Second person (you): **mày**

Third person (he/she): **nó** (referring to a person as "it," making them subhuman)

Knowing these pronouns is your first step to having street cred in street Vietnamese. These terms, although basic and known by schoolyard children in Vietnam, are seldom known by foreigners, even foreigners quite good with Vietnamese, because they are not used in formal or "respectable" contexts. However, I have seen a guidebook for sale that taught tao and mày as the terms to use "in informal situations" -- either a cruel practical joke, or, more likely, the result of a guidebook writer who is just "researching" from a dictionary.

9x youth slang

American culture has "millennials." In Vietnam, we have "9x," meaning people born in the 1990s. 9x correspondent Elly humbly reporting in for duty. Americans think their world was transformed in the 1990s; let me assure you Vietnam was transformed much more. Economic reform started in 1986, and post-1990 Vietnam looked very little like pre-1986 Vietnam. That's only Vietnam's particular history of change in that decade, but add to that the worldwide patterns of change during that decade that you likely experienced in your own country -- including but not only limited to the internet -- and you can see what I'm talking about. So the 9x generation is seen as the forefront of a modernizing Vietnam, in a somewhat ironic reversal of how in previous Vietnamese generations, young people were seen as the "front" or "vanguard" of Communist revolution.

The stereotypes of 9x people in Vietnam are not much different from the stereotypes about young people in any culture: 9x people (supposedly) don't respect tradition, don't respect traditional hierarchies and family structures, are too materialistic, are too into electronics and technology, are too interested in sex, are into foreign culture like Hollywood movies and pop music, and so on. Pretty standard stuff.

Ăn chùa
Literal meaning: to eat at a Buddhist temple
Real meaning: to mooch free food from somebody
Explanation: Buddhist temples give free food to the poor. Additionally, this is a pun on the nearly identical expression "Ăn chưa?" which means "Have you eaten yet?" "Chưa" means "yet" while "chùa" means a Buddhist temple. Someone can answer the question "Ăn chưa?" with a cheeky reply of "Ăn chùa."

Ảo tưởng sức mạnh
Literal meaning: imaginary power
Real meaning: overconfidence

Bão
Literal meaning: a storm
Real meaning: A Vietnamese flash mob. Going out in a crowd of motorcycles or sometimes cars, making a lot of noise at night and driving fast and recklessly, often when celebrating a public holiday or especially a sports victory. These "storms" are a growing social problem or social outlet (depending how you see it) in Vietnam's major cities. The police's inability to stop youth "storms" has been seen as a major challenge to police power.

Bấm nút, biến!
Literal meaning: press the button, launch!
Real meaning: rudely telling someone to get lost, fuck off, take a long walk off a short pier
Example: Mày nói nhiều quá, bấm nút biến!
You talk way too much! Press the button, launch!

Bánh bèo
Literal meaning: rice cake
Real meaning: a bimbo, a useless girl
Explanation: Rice cakes are white colored, and Vietnamese bimbos (or just Vietnamese pretty girls) prize themselves for having white skin; additionally, rice cakes have no taste or substance, indeed like those bimbo girls!

Bộ tay
Literal meaning: hands tied
Real meaning: "I can't deal with this" or "there's nothing more I can do" -- either seriously or jokingly. Often used jokingly when someone makes an outlandish or ridiculous statement.
Extra: Some young people jokingly say chân tay, tied feet, to mean the same thing.

Chai
Literal meaning: a bottle
Real meaning: one million Vietnamese dong
Example: Tao mua cái điện thoại này 7 chai.
I paid 7 " bottles" for this cellphone.
Explanation: An slurred pronunciation of the near-homonym triệu, the

standard word for million. This slang term also makes use of the standard Vietnamese "youth slang" method of using "ch" where the correct spelling is "tr" -- maybe similar to English-speaking youth using *z* to make a plural instead of *s*.

Chó vàng
Literal meaning: golden dog
Real meaning: traffic policeman
Explanation: Saigon traffic police officers wear beige uniforms, and are infamous for requesting some "gold" in exchange for not issuing a traffic citation. Additionally, in Vietnamese culture, dogs are seen as parasitical and predatory, not really "man's best friend" other than with perhaps the youngest and most urbanized and Westernized Vietnamese people.

Dân chợ búa
Literal meaning: people from the market
Real meaning: rough people, thuggish people, rough-mannered people, street type people -- note similarity with "**Đồ con buôn,**" another pejorative term related to merchants.

Di chợ
Literal meaning: go to the market
Real meaning: choose from a restaurant menu

Đu dây điện
Literal meaning: hang on an electric wire
Real meaning: to have one's head in the clouds

Đập đá
Literal meaning: rock mining
Real meaning: using crystal meth (methamphetamines)
Not to be confused with: A tough or unbreakable consumer item, especially a phone or a motorcycle, usually old, though, and unbreakable, can also be referred to as "đập đá," something so durable that you can mine rocks with it .

Đặt gạch
Literal meaning: to place a brick
Real meaning: to reserve something in advance

Dìm hàng
Literal meaning: to immerse or to dip
Real meaning: to defame or bully someone, especially online

Đo đường
Literal meaning: to measure the street (by lying down on it)
Real meaning: to be involved in a motorcycle accident

Dư xăng
Literal meaning: plenty of fuel
Real meaning: to be very capable of overcoming an obstacle, maybe slightly similar to the English term "cooking with gas"

Hầm bà lằng
Literal meaning: nuclear meltdown
Real meaning: A bunch of crap, a bunch of unwanted or low-quality things -- can be used about possessions, food, emotions, anything.

GATO
Literal meaning: Ghen Ăn Tức Ở, immediately overcome by envy
Real meaning: being very envious

Hư cấu
Literal meaning: work of fiction
Real meaning: person who tells tall tales, bullshitter

Khô máu
Literal meaning: dried blood
Real meaning: broke, poor

Làm màu
Literal meaning: make colors
Real meaning: show off

Lấy thịt đè người
Literal meaning: throw human meat
Real meaning: use one's big physical size to intimidate or assault people, also in sports or boxing, used to emphasize that a competitor is only using

his physical size, and not skill or athleticism

Mày hả bưởi!
Literal meaning: you grapefruit!
Real meaning: Strong positive affirmation and agreement, like "yeah, alright, that's what I'm talking about!" or "you can say that again!" No one seems to know the origin of this phrase, although perhaps it's playing on the similar sound of bưởi (grapefruit) and vui (enjoyable).

Năm năm không tám (5508)
Literal meaning: five five zero eight
Real meaning: smelly or slovenly person
Explanation: 5508 is an almost exact homonym for **năm năm không tắm**, five years no bathing.

Ném đá
Literal meaning: throwing rocks
Real meaning: criticizing, especially online

Ngắm gà khỏa thân
Literal meaning: nude chicken watching
Real meaning: dead
Explanation: Boiled ("naked") chicken is a traditional offering made at the graves and shrines of deceased relatives; dead people are colloquially said to be "watching naked chickens."

Nồi cơm điện
Literal meaning: rice cooker
Real meaning: motorcycle helmet

Ngựa sắt
Literal meaning: iron horse
Real meaning: bicycle, similar to the meaning of the American term "iron horse" used for cars

Nhà mày sáng nhất đêm nay!
Literal meaning: Your house will be brightly illuminated (on fire) tonight!
Real meaning: A threat: I'm going to fuck your shit up. Remember that

traditional Vietnamese village houses were made of highly flammable materials, and there were no professional firefighters in a traditional village.

Nói như đúng rồi!
Literal meaning: it has been said exactly correctly
Real meaning: used sarcastically, to tell someone that what they said is completely wrong

Quăng bom
Literal meaning: throwing bombs
Real meaning: to brag and show off, to bullshit

Quẩy
Literal meaning: to stir
Real meaning: to party, to attend a party, may sometimes imply sexual activity

Sáng nắng chiều mưa
Literal meaning: morning sun evening rain
Real meaning: moody, usually said of a woman

Sao phải xoắn?
Literal meaning: Why are you all twisted up?
Real meaning: don't worry so much, don't be so serious

Trâu bò
Literal meaning: cattle
Real meaning: someone who can endure many hardships; being trâu bò is seen as a defining feature of the older generations of Vietnamese, and this piece of slang plays upon widely held uncertainty about whether the materially comfortable new generations (like me) can endure hardships.

Tự sướng
Literal meaning: masturbation
Real meaning: selfie photo

Túm bảy túm ba
Literal meaning: take seven, take three

Real meaning: people talking about silly or ridiculous things, talking nonsense

Uống lộn thuốc hả?
Literal meaning: Did you take the wrong medicine?
Real meaning: WTF?! What's wrong with you?

Viêm cánh
Literal meaning: armpit inflammation
Real meaning: strong body odor

Xe chạy bằng cơm
Literal meaning: vehicle operated by rice
Real meaning: used to jokingly refer to walking or bicycling as transportation

Swearing: the bad stuff

Swearing in Vietnamese starts with the obligatory use of the rude pronouns **tao**, **mày**, and **nó**. I have heard of foreigners attempting to swear at taxi drivers and calling them a formal term of address for an uncle -- since the taxi driver is an older man, right? It sounds ridiculous in Vietnamese to combine swearing with the formal terms of address, but maybe you can get away with it as your own innovation. It's kind of like in English saying, "fuck you, my dear sir," or "suck my dick, your majesty." I could see it working in certain contexts. But it's not the usual structure of swearing, especially in Vietnamese, you denote so much about your context by the pronouns you use.

Other than pronouns, the basic building blocks of Vietnamese swearing are quite similar to those of any language's swearing: sex (fucking), dirtiness, death, mothers, and, perhaps surprisingly to Americans, dogs. Fucking is **đụ**, a filthy disgusting person is **đồ** (which is a common way to address the person you're insulting), a rude way to call a man is **thằng**, the rude way to refer to dying is **chết** (being polite, you would say đi xa meaning go far away), mother is **má** (Saigon) or **mẹ** (Hanoi), and a dog is **chó**. With those building blocks, you're all set. One way of coming up with Vietnamese swearing is just to mix up some imagery about someone's mother, a dog, death, and sex. That's what most serious Vietnamese profanity comes down to. Maybe the biggest difference between Vietnamese and English swearing is our prominent use of dog imagery. English does a little bit of this with the term "bitch," but it doesn't go as far as Vietnamese.

If you're wondering about body parts, they are not used that often in Vietnamese swearing. For the sake of completeness however, in street slang, a penis is called cặc or cu or chim (the first term is an obvious homonym, while the other two literally mean "bird"; think of "showing the bird" in English), and a vagina is called a bướm (butterfly, also a near-homonym for a sail) if you're not being very vulgar or *lồn* if you're being very vulgar. But while in English you might insult your friend by calling him "dick" or "pussy," in Vietnamese, people would just look at you like "huh?" if you attempted to use those insults -- as words for body parts aren't used as insults n Vietnamese swearing.

Cài lồn gì thế (CLGT)
Literal meaning: This vagina is what? (*lồn* is vagina)
Real meaning: WTF just happened?!

Chết mẹ luôn!
Literal meaning: mother always dead
Real meaning: inserted into speech for additional emphasis, like "fuckin'" is used in English.

Chết vì lồn (CVL) / Chết vì cac (CVC)
Literal meaning: killed by vagina (lồn) or penis (cac)
Real meaning: Someone who is boy-crazy or girl-crazy, obsessed with a romantic partner, is said to have "died by the vagina" or "died by the penis"

Chó chết

Literal meaning: dead dog
Real meaning: all-around insult, like "you piece of shit"

Chó đẻ
Literal meaning: a dog's offspring
Real meaning: a disagreeable person, an asshole; similar to English meaning of "son of a bitch," but in Vietnamese, chó đẻ is equally applied to men and women, implying that their parents didn't raise them correctly, or their parents themselves are "dogs."

Con mẹ nó (CMN)
Literal meaning: its mother
Real meaning: Used for emphasis, no specific meaning, similar to putting "fucking" in front of a noun in English

Cút đi
Literal meaning: depart
Real meaning: fuck off, go fuck yourself, get out of here -- very strong, and usually said in anger

Đéo
Literal meaning: Sexual intercourse
Real meaning: A street-tough way to say no. Like "fuck no" or "hell no" in English.
Extra: To avoid saying " đéo," which is strong, people sometimes say " ứ" or " đứ" or " éo."

Đồ con buôn
Literal meaning: trader, hustler, greedy merchant
Real meaning: disreputable, untrustworthy
Explanation: Đồ, which literally means "dirty," is a commonly used starting word for insults; in such insults it means "you dirty thing" or "you piece of shit." As for the rest of the term, I've heard of Westerners who assume that the association between traders and being disreputable comes from Communism -- but no, Vietnamese culture had the simultaneous love and hate of trading and business as long as anyone remembers, certainly back to the Chinese colonial times, long before the Vietnamese Communist Party.

Đồ não phẳng
Literal meaning: Flat brain person
Real meaning: A very stupid person

Đồ óc chó!
Literal meaning: dog-brained
Real meaning: idiot

Đụ má mày (online/SMS abbreviation: ĐMM) or Đụ má (ĐM)
Literal meaning: Fuck (your) mother
Real meaning: Same as "fuck you" in English; used as an insult even if you don't literally have romantic intentions toward the person's mother. Can also be used to express surprise, like "fuck me!" might be in English.
Explanation: This is the most classic South Vietnamese all-around curse

and insult. If you are a tourist in Saigon, perhaps you can hear it said around you, especially by an upset taxi drivers.

Đừng khóc mà (ĐKM)
Literal meaning: stop crying
Real meaning: emphasizing that the speaker is superior to the listener, like "I just pawned you"

Sủa
Literal meaning: barking
Real meaning: bullshitting, talking too much

Thiếu muối!
Literal meaning: lack of salt
Real meaning: rude way to accuse someone of being mentally handicapped, meaning that they're very stupid
Explanation: Traditionally Vietnamese medical beliefs are that the brain requires salt to function, and mental disability comes from a salt deficiency. People say that this belief comes from the salty taste of pig brains, which used to be a commonly eaten dish in Vietnam.

Types of people

Attribute it to our Chinese, French, and Russian colonial histories: we Vietnamese people love to categorize everything and especially everybody. Here are some of the "stock characters" you'll encounter in Vietnamese slang culture.

Ăn lông ở lỗ
Literal meaning: fur-hide-eaters (cavemen, savages)
Real meaning: uncivilized, impolite people, people with dirty homes

Bà tám
Literal meaning: Mrs. Eight
Real meaning: blabbermouth, busybody, chatty person, always said of a woman
Explanation: It's uncertain where this comes from. Perhaps it's a homonym and pun for ba tám, three eight, which has a similar meaning to "busybody woman" in some Chinese dialects.

Bán xà bông
Literal meaning: shampoo seller
Real meaning: gay men
Explanation: A spoonerism : "bán xà bông" (shampoo seller) comes " bóng xà ban" (wandering gay man). Also alludes to the stereotype of gay men working in hair salons.

Bao Công
Literal meaning: a character in Chinese legends who happens to have dark skin
Real meaning: a dark-skinned person (usually used for dark-skinned Vietnamese people, although I suppose it could also be used for dark-skinned foreigners, e.g. Africans)

Chân dài
Literal meaning: long legs
Real meaning: beautiful girl, especially a promotional model
Extra: sometimes a promotional model is called **PG**, pronounced as it would be in English, "promotion girl" -- this can mean anyone from a

magazine model to a tradeshow model to a teenage girl paid to stand in front of a store and "look pretty." Another term for this kind of girl, also pronounced exactly as in English: **hotgirl** (one word).

Cụ non
Literal meaning: premature aging
Real meaning: a young person who is preternaturally mature; generally a positive term

Đầu tôm
Literal meaning: Shrimp head
Real meaning: shallow, uninteresting person

Dân quận 4 or Q4 dân
Literal meaning: people who are from Saigon's Quan 4
Real meaning: thugs, street criminals, rough people
Explanation: Saigon's Quan 4 is traditionally (less so now) the domain of criminals. Why? Perhaps this relates to Vietnamese culture, just like Chinese culture, disliking the number 4 (tetraphobia) -- only criminals would want to live in quan number 4, or perhaps the other way around, anyone living in quan number 4 is regarded as a lowlife. In modern Vietnamese numbers (as opposed to the Cantonese numbers previously used in Vietnam), the word for "four" doesn't mean anything bad, but still, we often avoid saying it directly, because of our Sinitic cultural background.

Giang hồ
Literal meaning: from Chinese, the same as "gung ho"
Real meaning: street thugs

Mỏ nhọn
Literal meaning: pointy beak
Real meaning: quick-witted, well-spoken, witty

Nhà quê
Literal meaning: countryside
Real meaning: redneck, bumpkin, hick
Explanation: There is a strong urban-rural divide in Vietnam, and people living in cities consider themselves worlds apart from rural people. This

term is perhaps the most common one used to deride rural Vietnamese people, sometimes jokingly (such as when someone acts naive or unfashionable) or sometimes in a real derogatory way. The term can be used as a noun applied to a person or to a place, or as an adjective.
Extra: In reverse, **quê nhà** means hometown. Of course, people who believe their hometowns to be rural backwoods places have a lot of fun combining the terms **quê nhà** and n**hà quê.**

Quái xế
Literal meaning: Monster drivers
Real meaning: drag racers, street racers, reckless drivers
Explanation: Yes, the Fast And Furious movies are huge in Vietnam, and yes, teenage boys try to emulate them on their motorcycles in Saigon, becoming "monster drivers."

Tây ba lô
Literal meaning: Western backpack
Real meaning: backpacker, a low-class Westerner in Vietnam -- can be used pejoratively to emphasize that someone is dirty and low-class, or neutrally to mean a young traveler

Thị Nở
Literal meaning: A physically unattractive female character in the novel "Chí Phèo" by Nam Cao.
Real meaning: a physically unattractive woman, an ugly girl

Thỏ đế
Literal meaning: rabbit
Real meaning: coward
Explanation: in Vietnamese fairy tales, rabbits represent cowardice -- just as in English, you call a coward a "chicken" (by the way, be careful if you try to directly translate that English term, because in Vietnamese slang, a "chicken" is a prostitute)

Thớt
Literal meaning: cutting board
Real meaning: a host or emcee, especially for a talk show or a debate, especially used online to refer to hosts or moderators of discussion forums.

Trái bảo
Literal meaning: secret boy
Real meaning: male prostitute
Extra: This term also plays on the term **bảo trái**, which means financially supporting a man. In fact, Vietnamese is full of word-pairs where reversing the order changes the meaning, sometimes in a comical way.

Trẻ trâu
Literal meaning: buffalo youth
Real meaning: misbehaving youth, little punks

Trương Phi
Literal meaning: a character in Chinese legends, known for his hot temper
Real meaning: hot-tempered, hothead

Xã hỏi đến
Literal meaning: dark society
Real meaning: mafia, gangsters; here "dark" just means subterfuge and hidden, illegal things, but I know some Americans automatically think it refers to skin color, which isn't the case here.

Business

Don't be fooled by Vietnam's nominal Communism. Vietnam is a highly commercial culture. Business is our business. And business also has some colorful vocabulary.

Bao...
Literal meaning: covered
Real meaning: guaranteed to meet an advertising claim, term usually seen on outdoor advertisements
Example: Cơm bao no đây! Giá bao rẻ luôn!
Meal guaranteed to make you full! Price guaranteedt to always be cheap!

Chém
Literal meaning: to behead
Real meaning: to cheat in business, especially used for merchants cheating customers
Example: Đừng mua đồ chỗ đó, nó chém lắm!
 Don't go shopping there, they'll behead you!

Cò
Literal meaning: heron (bird)
Real meaning: middleman, dealmaker, broker

Con ông cháu cha (COCC)
Literal meaning: grandson of his grandpa and son of his dad
Real meaning: favored son, daddy's boy, someone who reached their high position through nepotism and connections, especially in government

Nhà nghèo
Literal meaning: the poorhouse, a home for the indigently poor in Vietnamese tradition
Real meaning: bankrupt or unsuccessful business venture

Phong bì
Literal meaning: envelope
Real meaning: bribe (used as a noun or verb)
Explanation: A common gift (for a birthday or any other event) in

Vietnam is money in an envelope, following the Chinese tradition. Bribes might or might not be literally given in envelopes, but everyone in Vietnam knows that envelopes have money inside, and symbolize bribery. In fact, while in the West, an envelope might be used to surreptitiously disguise money, in Vietnam, it is said that bribe givers prefer *not* to use an envelope, because an envelope signals much too obviously that bribery is afoot.

Taxi dù
Literal meaning: parachuting taxi
Real meaning: dishonest taxi
Explanation: A parachuting taxi is seen as one that does "hit and run," cheating people and then disappearing, as if it had dropped in by parachute.

Xù
Literal meaning: wavy, unstable
Real meaning: evasive of a debt, evading creditors, running away from a financial obligation
Explanation: This is most likely a pun on **xu**, which is the unit of money equal to 1/100th of 1 VND (like a penny for Americans). **Xu** are no longer in use, because even 1 VND is worth very little, so there's no need to subdivide it further -- but we do sometimes talk about **xu**.
Example: Thằng bạn tao xù mất 200k của tao rồi.
That guy "was wavy" about 200,000 of mine.

Love, sex, relationships

Perhaps in every culture, love, sex, and relationships are the richest source of colorful slang. Who wants to say "he inserted his penis in my vagina" when you could say.... well, something more colorful, or at least less obvious! We Saigonese people have a lot of these kinds of expressions, although I can't say I've personally had a chance to use many of them. On the other hand, I can't say that I haven't used any of them. Wink wink, right?

Ăn cơm or ăn phó
Literal meaning: eat rice / eat noodles
Real meaning: be with one's spouse / have an outside affair
Explanation: This dichotomy comes from the Southern Vietnamese belief that rice is a primary meal, and noodles are something "extra" or "on the side."

Ăn cơm trước kẻng
Literal meaning: eat rice before the bell rings
Real meaning: premarital sex

Áo mưa
Literal meaning: Raincoat
Real meaning: Condom (note that in Vietnam, condoms are associated with prostitution)

Cây sĩ
Literal meaning: Strong tree
Real meaning: Hopeless romantic, forever in love with someone who doesn't return their love. Usually male.

Còn ghế
Literal meaning: crab
Real meaning: girlfriend
Explanation: most likely comes from the similar sounding còn gai, meaning girl.

Đấu kiếm
Literal meaning: Swordfight
Real meaning: gay sex

Đứng đường
Literal meaning: Street standing
Real meaning: prostitution
Explanation: it's particularly catchy because it sounds almost like the same word repeated twice

Gà móng đỏ
Literal meaning: Chicken with red claws
Real meaning: prostitute
Explanation: In many East Asian languages, chickens are associated with prostitution. And traditionally in Vietnam, makeup and nail polish were associated with "bad girls" and especially prostitutes.

Gấu
Literal meaning: Bear
Real meaning: boyfriend, girlfriend, lover

Hai phải
Literal meaning: two methods
Real meaning: bisexual (usually said of men)
Explanation: Likely inspired by the homonymic English term "hi-fi," which, if you are around my age and need an explanation, referred to high-end audio around the 1970s and 1980s.

Kiếm chút cháo
Literal meaning: eat a little bit of porridge
Real meaning: "get some action" sexually, have some introductory sexual activity, often early in the relationship

Phi công trẻ lái máy bay bà già
Literal meaning: Young pilot flying an old airplane
Real meaning: A young man romantically involved with an older woman.

Quay tay
Literal meaning: Hands spinning

Real meaning: male masturbation
Extra: Female masturbation is **chà đĩa** (spinning records)

Trai quẹo
Literal meaning: not straight men/ bent men
Real meaning: Gay men
Example: Mày có thể đoán được thằng nào quẹo trong đám đó không?
Can you tell which one is bent in that buch of guys?
Extra: opposite to " trai quẹo" we have "trai thẳng" – Straight men.

Xếp hình
Literal meaning: Playing Lego
Real meaning: sexual intercourse, because Lego blocks involve fitting clips into holes
Example: Mày với con đó có xếp hình tối qua không?
Did you play Lego with her last night?

High school

Yes, Vietnamese high school is mostly about test scores; social life and sports are not prominent parts of the experience, although we do (and I did) longingly watch American high school movies!

Cây gậy
Literal meaning: A stick
Real meaning: score a 1 (Vietnamese schools usually give grades 1 to 5, similar to F to A for Americans)

Địa
Literal meaning: land, soil
Real meaning: copy answers from a fellow student nearby, because you pretend you're "looking at the ground"

Lụi
Literal meaning: to stab
Real meaning: doing multiple choice tests randomly without thinking

Phao
Literal meaning: buoys
Real meaning: Cheating materials, hidden notes

Trứng vịt
Literal meaning: duck egg
Real meaning: receive a zero score

Tủ đè
Literal meaning: get hit by a cabinet door
Real meaning: flunk a test
Extra: People say " học tủ" – study the cabinet (Study one particular part of the content which will appear in a test), and if things went wrong then you got hit by the cabinet (tủ đè).

Tu luyện
Literal meaning: prepare for monkhood
Real meaning: study intensely

Printed in Great Britain
by Amazon